Squall

*Poems in the Voice of
Mary Shelley*

Michael Mirolla, editor
David Moratto , cover and interior design
judith S bauer, cover image: *Earth, I want promises*
judith S bauer, interior illustrations
Guernica Editions Inc.
287 Templemead Drive, Hamilton (ON), Canada L8W 2W4
2250 Military Road, Tonawanda, N.Y. 14150-6000 U.S.A.
www.guernicaeditions.com

Distributors:
Independent Publishers Group (IPG)
600 North Pulaski Road, Chicago IL 60624
University of Toronto Press Distribution,
5201 Dufferin Street, Toronto (ON), Canada M3H 5T8
Gazelle Book Services, White Cross Mills
High Town, Lancaster LA1 4XS U.K.

First edition.
Printed in Canada.

Legal Deposit—First Quarter
Library of Congress Catalog Card Number: 2019946613
Library and Archives Canada Cataloguing in Publication
Title: Squall : poems in the voice of Mary Shelley / Chad Norman.
Other titles: Poems in the voice of Mary Shelley
Names: Norman, Chad, author.
Series: Essential poets ; 274.
Description: Series statement: Essential poets series ; 274
Identifiers: Canadiana 20190155116 | ISBN 9781771835176 (softcover)
Classification: LCC PS8577.O469 S78 2020 | DDC C811/.54—dc23

*for Ana Rosa,
another woman I am filled with
and taught by.*

Contents

Mary Shelley's Tempest — *George Elliott Clarke* . . . . *xi*

This Parting The Earth Whispers, 1822 . . . . *3*

The Laws Of Italy, 1822 . . . . *5*

The Reflection Where Time Floats, 1822 . . . . *7*

The Unknown One, 1822 . . . . *11*

The Physical Tribe, 1822 . . . . *15*

  In memory of Dr. Poignand, my mother's last doctor *15*

  In memory of a doctor from a dream. *16*

  In memory of Dr. Vacca, sea & climate his cure-alls *17*

  In memory of Dr. Henry Cline, eminent young surgeon *20*

  In memory of Dr. Boiti, one out of the lot I'll laud. *23*

  In memory of Dr. Fordyce, criminal & family favourite. *25*

  In memory of Dr. Aglietti, perhaps still lost in Venice *29*

  In memory of Dr. Polidori, our ghostly summer in Geneva . . *31*

The Calm Murderer, 1822 . . . . *35*

Last Night Of The Elopement, 1822 . . . . *39*

The Raffish, 1821 . . . . *41*

Teresa Of The Tower, 1821. . . . . *42*

The Nigredo, 1820 . . . . *45*

Elena, 1820 . . . . *46*

A Room In Pisa, 1820. . . . . *47*

A Difficult Companion, 1819 . . . . *51*

A Grim Depletion, 1819 . . . . *54*

William, 1819 . . . . *56*

Clara, 1818 . . . . *58*

After Reading The 3rd Canto of Byron's *Childe Harold*, 1817 . . *60*

Dedication Revisited, 1817. . . . . *62*

The Prosperous Friction, 1816. . . . . *65*

A Hymn For A Hymn, 1816 . . . . *67*

The Unnamed Daughter, 1815 . . . . *68*

A Season At Bishopsgate, 1815 . . . . *70*

In The Dim Limbo, 1814 . . . . *72*

The Choice Revisited, 1814 . . . . *74*

The Mule, 1814 . . . . *77*

Promises At The St. Pancras Churchyard, 1814 . . . . *81*

No Other Heaven, 1812 . . . . *83*

Acknowledgements *87*

About the Author *89*

About the Illustrator *89*

Other Works By Chad Norman *91*

Mary Shelley's Tempest

For Jaime Augusto Shelley

What if the *lady*—Jane Austen's contemporary—who conceived the world's most intriguing modern monster (Doc Frankenstein's creature)—was also a proto-suffragette, precursor-feminist, and, simultaneously, much to her chagrin, wedded to a narcissist poet, whose liberalism urged on his libertinism? How would such a woman think? What would she say about her majuscule Romantic dilemma and miniscule romantic predicament? Such are the questions that Chad Norman pursues in his act (and art) of sympathetic re-animation: *Squall: Poems in the Voice of Mary Shelley.*

What have we here, in this narrative, this assembly of dramatic monologues? Well, Norman presents—in flashback—the musings of Shelley (1797-1851), positioned on a Philip Glass-abstract "beach" (historically, the strand at Viareggio, Italy), lamenting the death-by-water of her radical—sometimes caddish—husband, Percy Bysshe Shelley (1792-1822), and recalling a coupling that was, for both, a love-match, but harassed by PBS's first—and spurned—wife and creditors and lawyers. Norman lets Mary Shelley revise PBS's political attitudes. Yes, her hubby inked exquisite verse about doing-the-right-thing and dreaming-the-right-governance (Utopia), but his personal life exhibited much of the reverse. In a sense, then, the widow Shelley corrects the immor(t)al Shelley.

Each poem herein begins with Mary on a beach, a box in her possession. We should guess that the box contains PBS's heart—the one part of him that would not burn when his cadaver was hoisted upon a waterside pyre. Thus, the symbolic box is a treasure chest, but one that Mary treats as if it were her dead husband's physical chest—his trunk (as it were); so she rests beside it, handles it, and is never far (or divorced) from it.

Located on this beach, Mary registers, "the aimless quality of the sea," a phrase that could also refer to PBS's peripatetic and meandering life, that ends so dismally prematurely. One thinks of the widowed Jacqueline Kennedy commenting on the loss of JFK: "All his bright light—gone from the world." If PBS was both beneficiary and victim of his "whimsied mind," Mary yet had to face, stoically, the wayward results of his wrong-headed thinking and deeds: "Sadly," Norman has her say, "I found you beautiful." That admiration permitted her to endure, "the blasted cell of a love / our lives began to pace." Arguably, Norman's Mary foreshadows Margaret Atwood's Susanna Moodie: Both had to plant their deceased offspring in foreign soil. Painfully though, Mary's loss is due partly to PBS's "benign neglect" (Daniel Patrick Moynihan's phrase from another context) of their offspring, perhaps due to a predilection for abstract *Imagination* rather than attending to infants' bodily needs.

Despite adultery, debt, disease, and drownings (including of PBS's first wife, a suicide), Mary yet recognizes, "There is no other Heaven ...," presumably, than the here-and-now and the love that she lived with PBS:

> I gaze at the edge of Italy,
> unable to forget
> we shared all
> we dared to,
> the effort holy,
> enough ....

Surely, *Memory* is half *Nostalgia*, so that what was bitter becomes beautiful:

> memory saves:
> the undulant hair,
> the open mouth,
> the muted bubbles ....

Lost is PBS — the genius incarcerated ultimately in lethal liquid. Still, Mary did know — has known — *Love*:

> the dually-sired girl I was
> sat wryly open-thighed,
> exposing my eager whitened cleft
> done with the dark red drop
> found in the chair, by the fingers
> I knew I needed to taste ....

Norman's Mary Shelley reminds me of French filmmaker Jean Rollin's daemon-nymphs, his beach-haunting Ophelias, often fanged, who, rather than drowning themselves, prefer to set boats and sailors alight or to see them entombed in coffins set adrift at sea — like so many bottles with dead letters within, the detritus of romance stories remaindered or pulped. Then again, Rollin's cinema merges eroticism and horror; he's Tinto Brass offering sensual elegance and Quentin Tarantino rendering surreal gore. There's a tinge of both in Norman — or, rather, in his version of Mary Shelley's self-portraiture .... Even so, the style — the diction — of Norman's Shelleyan verse is clearly Canadian, given his delight in abstract adjectives and/or airy-fairy nouns coupled with physical nouns or set to enact physical verbs.

Whether or not Norman has read American poet Robert Cooperman's dramatic monologues, *In the Household of Percy Bysshe Shelley* (1993), one should leaf through his book in tandem with Norman's *Squall*. A second fellow-traveller text, so to speak, is work by Basil Bunting, who's also keen to blend the vernacular and the oracular: See *Briggflatts* (1966). I recommend Bunting because Norman's tone—or atmosphere—is that of the séance. In *Squall*, we witness Mary Shelley in communion with her own soul ....

I've known Chad Norman for thirty years. He's written fine work before, but *Squall* is one of his best. Kudos to him for giving a vital woman voice. Certainly, Mary Wollstonecraft Shelley is rendered brilliantly herein, both as the creator of a masterpiece (*Frankenstein*, 1818) and as the critical curator of a spouse-maker's legacy.

George Elliott Clarke
Parliamentary Poet Laureate (2016 & 2017)
11 *Messidor* (1 *juillet*) mmxvi

The last voyage of Ariel, or Don Juan.

This parting the earth whispers.

This Parting The Earth Whispers, 1822

Mary with a cheek to the land;
a small sealed box by her face

I

I have rested on
the bosom of a man
the sea consoled
as if it were the wife
he forgot
in the centre of his final wish.
To enter the Earth,
by the waves' bright gate
willing to hinder
the lungs' helpless cycles,
boat or no boat,
for the squall's facile rescue.

II

Rhythms of this planet
entertain one ear;
from the imagination's reach
his heartbeat begins
to roll about in the other,
broken by the sea's tease,
a damp tapping gust
eager to play the Past.

III

Deceive my cheek no more!
Earth,
I want promises ....

The Laws Of Italy, 1822

Mary at the sea's edge;
a small sealed box in her hands

By the guilty sea
I hold the heart of Shelley
as my body moves to view
the hated distance,
the way weather chars
the flower's new petal,
under the window he loved to be in
or behind; the pyres
long after the laws,
shadows of fires
built for the bodies
the squall knew a short night,
pools where the sun leads
my eyes back into his,
the stare, I, Mary,
fell into gladly at Bracknell.

We, decisive & damned,
began what led this beach
to be the first reality
our lives must relinquish,
a drowning now between us,
no guesses were necessary;
the thievish waves
attempt to console my conference
as the heart prepares
to serve another extraction.

Percy! Percy!
My knees on this innocent shore,
my tears on the sand
moving like cries in a crowd
the mind meanders

far off to where the Past
was pure when the poems & children
made the days a haven.

The insects,
shadows the clouds share,
dive in heat
the day decisions mean
you live bodiless in my body,
gone under forever,
as this loud hour brings a dusk
willing to save our farewell,
afloat in the orange foam.

The Reflection Where Time Floats, 1822

Mary seated in grass by the sea;
a small sealed box at her foot

Heaven, heaven,
stop pretending to be the sky!

Whisper?
The Church has lost a voice,
still sinking,
the flames out & over,
Percy,
my nearby husband,
speaking up through
the divine learning fathoms,
unwanted by air,
the expulsive minds of England.

Look, see a time,
behind my veiled hair,
the Godless clouds
led his quill to revolt
as we were tender beside
a more silent shore,
the soft & pointed grass
against our backs
no greener than the tufts
surrounding my dress
unable to leave this body
since his bright hand
waved above the final goodbyes
I tried to bar.

Storms are thieves sent to replace thought.

For a first, my face,
verifies the colour of voids:
the sun,
his other equal,
searches to set on
the fated boat
docking after Byron & Leghorn.
Squall!
Define it?
Storms are thieves sent
to replace thought
like reminders tighten on wrists
resting in my lap —
what did he want?
Not this,
night parting us
in the pool's soft fading advice.

A day came for the face when it longed to be a mask.

The Unknown One, 1822

Mary crawling through the surf;
a small sealed box washed ashore

A day came for the face
when it longed to be a mask,
the gaunt mould
Death grants the mother
as her womb collapses,
to force the waters aboard
the blood's wise fear,
her fate for a future *you* gladly haunt.

Fortunately I saw
nor see no face,
no asking fingers,
the gasping finality
your recent siblings wore
in Rome & Venice.

Fortunately I was rescued
from intentions,
fatal, understood,
the hope of our last
to lead my life,
cold & closed,
off to end.

Neglect ...
whom I was to carry about instead!

And less weighted
meant the mother's watch
change from the child
to the saved woman,
emptied, encased,
profoundly eager to examine
the block of ice I owe;

the hands of my husband
red with excessive flow
caught in shreds of a shirt,
once white, & once warm.

My mother's last doctor.

The Physical Tribe, 1822

Mary lighting a fire on the beach;
a small sealed box on the dry kindling

I

In memory of Dr. Poignand, my mother's last doctor.

Above her station
there was a gender,
rough, arrogant, predictable,
and young,
an education skimming the placid Mind
they formed as a whole,
any care in being civilized & clean
left outside in the streets
she strolled only days
before the confinement was bribed,
how the midwife's presence
ends in insult,
jeer, & taunt,
the man of Medicine threatened
by her ancient prepared hands,
scrubbed, steaming,
held up to frame the face
mothers chose to meet their infants.
I see her forced from the room,
a witch.

II

In memory of a doctor from a dream.

Care became a misbegotten act
for my gender,
I stared into the eyes of my Age
& saw myself each short visit
he intended to be vigilant,
until his squinting began
to beguile thoughts I tried to follow,
while his hands were there,
the clenched exit
I kept clean for my child. ·

Daring Society,
you too fall open for the probe,
I see clearly as sleep
had me prone & placed—
what a disaster,
in one way,
& not in another;
sore trickery the mind saw
as a fine bore
kept my eyes sealed
to watch the *instrument*,
intentionally frigid,
float over the etched skin
his selfish tutored fingers held,
as dawn's prod
felt like a rescue,
chimes for my unsafe child.

III

In memory of Dr. Vacca, sea & climate, his cure-alls.

To have known everyone
worth knowing in Pisa,
as the new circle grew around us,
the Sociable, the Open-Minded,
the Cultivated,
all brought in to where
our wants became a world of mirth
I required,
distant from the stalking ailment
my Percy withstood,
tired of the opiate's vial,
the many climaxes glee allows
when one entertains the Self for a time,
too aware,
& too indulgent.

At the gathering
I flirted with "Europe's finest"
until his discourse fell
to the drivel of a fool,
the sublime echelons of Science
reliant on climate,
& Medicine,
the edacious tyke of his claim,
said to *trust*
the salt of the sea,
how the simple wave
carries the sun,
a daily cache of healing rays.
A complete wife at his side
wisely timed our rescue!
Such false hospitality
wore fast my thin patience,
a disaster's lull began to loom,
faces, hands, & eyes,
all circling when sleep
took up the cause to warn,
the night harsh & vocal,
low goading whispers
furious like those of a captor,
building in my mind
the return of doom's familiarity,
yet a pleasant dawn broke in,
set our plans for
a day of half-crowns & pistols.

The calamity of a collision
still unknown & frozen,
the maniacal dragoon
had not galloped into our party,
no insult wild & drunken,
no mad strike ending our
usual & playful afternoon —
how I wish to be seated
in that trailing carriage again,
witness to a wager
I knew to be our last,
the unalterable moment so far
from the charming doctor,
not quite ready to make it clear
the English friends of Byron
were no longer welcome
in a city where cold blood
coated the quiet pitch-fork.

IV

In memory of Dr. Henry Cline, eminent young surgeon.

Nothing is more required than
a fascinating disaster
during a 13 year old girl's
first eruption of eczema,
a blemished trial,
where the home changes
into a ship's deck
off the approaching coasts of Scotland,
the cure I took
after father no longer knew loneliness,
sold to him by
the unfriendly man I held my sick arm
out to before he spoke,
brought on our separation.

The *new* parent,
the woman after my brief wishful mother,
I could barely address
em-jay much less Mama;
like a leer on a face
I dare not forget,
or the old struggle
to reach a cordial frontier I knew
when forgiveness had to be sought,
my callow life changed
to rugged little riots,
tense events whereby I stood
my youth beside *her*,
the vicious child disguised as a wife.

And when he spoke,
my tilted father's trusty source
seemed briefed on
the plan for
another palliative seaside resort,
after all the promise of
Ramsgate's powers was held
sadly by another master of nature;
Scotland! Scotland!
I tired of the timed frequency
I heard of you,
the country prescribed
for my next education,
the antidote for more than
my *girlish troubles*.
Truce or no truce,
I set sail to deal with absence.

Among the many hands waving
the doleful waft of farewells,
one unforeseen face
rose from the rotund frenzy
—why then mother?
Why, as I preferred to glower,
penetrate those two men
with eyes meant to haunt?
My father dared not to miss a moment,
as for the faithful other,
heroic Cline,
I detected a weakness
for his own dirty boots.
As I do now,
& as I did then facing
the aimless calamity of the sea,
I quell that queer urge to blame.

V

In memory of Dr. Boiti, one out of the lot I'll laud.

All through the shrewd coupling
they careened from
the horde's sniping lips
to my lenient eye,
until the rapid moments ceased
to insult & inform,
moments I awoke into,
like the dawn into a storm
one night withstood,
moments my husband chose to chase
what his whimsied mind had clearly whetted
for the stepsister
I insisted be put to an employer.
Claire,
traitorous & close,
became the sheer foe.
Claire,
without a way,
a woman he alone wandered.
Out!
Her only direction,
our agitated circle reduced,
to daily tiffs,
snide rivalry,
her only direction,
out, out of my home,
out of my marriage,
sooner

this than more of
my unnecessary, badgered mind.
How unusual when it danced
in the belief of news
I raved over when
wishes flew like bright faces
with honest eyes,
faces the memory kept to send
into that dear anticipated day
lush with her leaving.

A new family.
A new city.
A new breath.
A new Italy.
Can it be,
this an hour of the visiting past,
when he removed what so ailed
& divided such able women,
one firm in the hope of domestic seclusion,
despite her aversion to
the folly of roles,
how it ends love.
And one,
taken away by the brave doctor,
a scheme for them
to arrange their chances,
as if his circle was taking in
the *other wanderer* I rightfully waived,
glad to end
the source of scandal
she knew she was.

VI

In Memory of Dr. Fordyce, the criminal & family favourite.

A visitor,
a welcome,
the first big fly arrived,
one berserk wing
hung from the body,
loud,
vicious invalid in flight
over sudden rays
the room held for her.

Mother,
my other Mary,
now full of no infant,
their red-wine ritual
sipped
as if her lost blood,
seeped
by the spent placenta,
could really be replaced.

Mother,
alone,
in a new confinement,
their handy puppies on hire,
the useless milk,
her loss of choice.

All this I knew from behind a door
like my hiding
as Coleridge raved his Mariner.

All this I knew when she left the smile
our family's culpable, medical choice,
him,
idiotically
presumed was his—
Mother,
I retain such an inescapable gift.

He chose to bury more of himself.

VII

In memory of Dr. Aglietti, perhaps still lost in Venice.

Francesco,
if this is what time brings,
my life now on one knee,
the motley pangs return
like the moments the Past bore them,
searing, robust,
anxious to lower the woman I'm left,
differing little from the mother
I was,
the day my tiny dead Clara
shook no more.

You were not to be found,
my Percy's crazed pursuit,
brought nothing
but his own catastrophic error,
our only daughter ill at Este,
his demand to travel,
his crass need to cover up
the lie left to deceive Byron,
his oath to an overcast sky,
daily, sequacious,
the tragic privacy of a fault.

Francesco,
if he took on the blame,
what Loss did not insist upon,
what I felt & still feel as a wife,
the long hapless course of bitterness,
may have been shared,
our child alive,
somewhere other than
the unmarked grave on the Lido's beach,
no tablet to say she's gone,
another lonely place
he chose to bury more of himself,
the infrequent fool
unable to avoid Death's avid toll,
like you
a man with a sown mind,
caught in crucibles then afoot.

You were not to be found.
This tidal memory
surrounded by timeless sand,
where the sea is beyond
my featured need to forget.

VIII

In memory of Dr. Polidori, & our ghostly summer in Geneva.

A regal cloud's roving shadow
seems to demand,
seems to colour the pert sand
with permission to thank you,
the secret love hidden so poorly,
the helpful arm almost held out
as I scaled the hills between our villas,
where the act of gallantry
left you the injured one,
those shy telling eyes
able to carry the embarrassment,
the lean ankle swelling
in my supple grasp,
the morning's ink
running down my fingers in
what was the sweat
our moment of care mixed
in the sun's cogent sheen:
hope in your veins,
set on some impossible liaison.

Where the act of gallantry left you the injured one.

Sadly, I found you beautiful,
in the air briefly
during the leap off the balcony,
& as a patient
after master Byron
broke from the automaton,
& brought you a pillow
& the cold water,
another curious act
to remind us,
or perhaps reanimate us,
both I welcomed & intuited,
as for you, confidant,
among our fluid youth,
the halting moment
hung in a moderate trust,
suspicion there at your side
outspent,
& suicide,
the galvanic whisper,
ready to relieve.

The sea's drifting conscience that sang over his final endless squints.

The Calm Murderer, 1822

> *Mary chin-deep in the sea;*
> *a small sealed box on a log washed ashore*

I

What proud music this new home plays,
notes grip the neck,
rude & rhythmic grasp set
to the sky's beat
aborted by the wave,
dark singer of
the sea's drifting conscience
that sang over his final endless squints:
the heretical gaze *you* held
before Loss began its strums.

II

A fog lifts
& lowers as dusk
joins the hidden horn.
No eye aboard
will mistake my face
for the seal's,
but beneath the bow
like a tempest in tow
he comes returned seemingly by
the insane tides of being alive,
part of the mist's aria
given to aid our embraces:
the motive *you* host
charms Love between its chants.

III

So, my Shelley,
The tugs I count must be proof,
touching a dream permits,
or the sly untuned ebb
eager to amuse my torn dress
for one performance,
the buoyant hoax,
in league with grief's wry lure
sent as a faint sinking mirage
the memory saves:
the undulant hair,
the open mouth,
the muted bubbles.

Our marriage was about us always eloping.

Last Night Of The Elopement, 1822

Mary facing the land;
a small sealed box at the sea's edge

Hands tilled
the rose's place of escape!
Our marriage was
about us always eloping ....

This night,
World,
streaking your colours
through star-racked galaxies,
what of the dark plain orbits?

Above
in the sun
a flame dies,
folding back the dust alight
over any hour
brought by clocks.

Trees go dry
straight across the day.

Nearer,
the moon
pries the hills,
grows from a branch where
night broods,
& stills.

On a day when shadows dared to be rooks.

The Raffish, 1821

Mary sitting in the sand;
a small sealed box on one knee

Detained,
missing my carriage,
on a day when shadows
dared to be rooks,
I was without a reason
for my English intolerance
—isn't it all sagas,
how fashion flaunts the Masses!

On the promenade among them
faces became dim and boring,
my mind sent forth a voice
loudening in words like "lowly"—
Pisa,
I shunted your showy peasants!

Curiosity brought about my stroll ...

Teresa Of The Tower, 1821

Mary napping beside a low fire;
a small sealed box under one hand

Today
the churlish memory
chose to
select a dream I partly failed
to put away the treasonous year
it ran a taunting course
like the amorphous clouds just now,
teasing,
in no hurry,
content to detain the sun,
steal from me
the Past's sympathetic return.
To deal with
the needs of a dream,
sanely,
dangling as usual,
a brave doubt between the dross & the pangs
I saw our bond
strangely become,
a crude shift he
sheathed in gainful concern,
triumphant too often,
late in those last years
we tried to redeem.
A sly attempt
to sate the jealousy
ushered the ruinous gait of

his spry craving
into the lunacy I knew well,
our sturdy losses steering us
easily toward the eventual Others
I revisit as their faces
peer from the clouds,
first his,
a gaze of slight & scurrility.
Then her,
leering from the dreamy pleasure-house
in a poem,
where she's to be lady of the solitude,
and, cagily together,
below the tower
they'd become One,
a lust,
a loss,
a lie,
alone on his swollen island.
All this paradise,
the jocose makings of
a steep deceit,
adrift like the cordial sorrow
I deftly shift within.
All this,
ill-bred,
scheming,
poorly imprisoned in a poem,
his beautiful wreck,
a silence where
their fictitious love attempts to speak ...
there was so much left to dream.

The fierce erect quill my tiny life lived within.

The Nigredo, 1820

Mary gathering driftwood for a fire;
a small sealed box in a circle of stones

Black,
I tell you the colour is a fiend,
and I do dare reveal
what a vigorous flirt,
after all
no other seduction won
my notions on the fertility of Death,
a morose season
I may soon abjure,
until then may night be suffice
unlike the Past,
when black
snuck from my mind
into the griefless light
of a room,
intending to violate
the brief valour
I woke to behold,
the aching ink
settled
in the page's kind silence,
the fierce erect quill
my tiny life lived within.

Elena, 1820

Mary lying in the sand;
a small sealed box on her hip

Sometimes I hide myself for Death
like secrets or an injury—
what day could it possibly be?
The sky & its blue are without a cloud,
cruel how it makes a way so soon
pulling a shadow on the nervous water,
like the memory of my near-drowned Shelley,
desperate, never so lost, yet successful
at keeping such a child news for others.
Others, the hidden circle for his letters,
held out by obeying a request of silence:
Must we ever speak of this child?
If so, may our dear Mary sleep in secrecy.
Such a child said to be of several wombs,
the ephemeral charge meant to churn mine,
a womb only months over the birth of a boy
I, like a cunning woman, released to rituals
known as breath, life beyond the age of three.
Three, mask & lies & mishap, Shelley let them
alter his ego, in the abrupt style of a deed
our insistence for Truth tore open at once,
still daring & unbelievably agape on this day.
He looks up from the sand where my finger
has stopped at the end of a smile I'm sure
such a child could call her father's, but
my finger resumes, leaving them for the sea,
the tide's first tired and maternal wave.

A Room In Pisa, 1820

Mary napping in grass by the sea;
a small sealed box under one hand

I

My Pisan moon grew
in night-shadows on the wall
as the dually-sired girl I was
sat wryly open-thighed,
exposing my eager whitened cleft,
done with the dark red drop
found on the chair, by the fingers
I knew I needed to taste.

II

When I scanned the scraping branch,
slowly tasting my inner time,
the open breath-dressed window
held the pleasant glowing room,
while the night taught the mind
how to recall each nail's creak.
No woman knew those rare notes
as she, that Mary, enlivened by quiet.

One brief joy I craved in private.

III

Words that I wrote saw nothing,
my favourite dress back in place
on the cool floor where two feet touched:
Casa Frassi, a new home for that room,
where our circle rested above the Arno
& I saw Exile in a corner with webs,
elated, crouched by the keyhole's crest
my finger traced after each noon rang.

IV

Songs of tired men rose from the river
to swirl within the wind of night,
as the blonde curtains shared both
I knew chuckle & cheer, unlike any
other moments my image was insignia
for the mirror finally less fulgent,
the sable face stoked by a smile
grown fitful, alone like a fire.

V

Inland gulls brought the hour dawn began,
wings full, as night left for the light
old tales tried to describe — one ray
claimed the one clean pane — a portal
I kept for the sun, my eyes, the game
my finger's shadow
in that bright circle on the bed.
One brief joy I craved in private.

VI

As I tapped the coals of that night
the scalding poker caught the grate,
a freak instant in the manner of music
caressed my receptive palm, loudly,
active while the room held a height
the keen day kindly fell from,
a cue to undress in the new heat,
stand bare, marvelled by a mood's rite.

A Difficult Companion, 1819

Mary kneeling face-down in the sand;
a small sealed box in grass by the beach

I

There was a name
for a man who had
thrown away God,
the foul ...,
no, I wouldn't dare call it a word,
or would I say
I used it often on him,
no I wouldn't turn to
such a woman of typical stirs.
His eyes helped me
to accept the strolls.
How he calmly held up
sly sisterly Claire's hand
to form the fist
made of his and hers,
the stare, or was it a glare,
one that spoke loudly
to an hour I heard
the two threads holding me upright snap.
Once as she grinned,
her eyes joining his
to inject the searing,
"Enjoy your ink! Sure Maie can't come?"
And once as he left first,

heedless,
no courage to comfort,
overlooking my eye-wide plea,
"I want someone to be happy with."
And as the door latched
I felt Pain enquire, "Why?"

II

Claire was one of her names.
& Claremont seemed the other —
I've always understood why Percy
insisted on her presence
in the carriage when dawn
led us from the London dirge,
and I stepped off at Calais
strongly in love,
as strong as dear sister,
with a man we knew to be married,
life-full, often in
the habit of sense and sensibility.

III

All that my journals tell
I planned to put to the pyre
my worry built,
to accommodate
a difficult companion,
that fierce she
now on the arm of Shelley,
out in the open, fearless,
by far the woman
my great mother
saw as Society's meed.
For us, the prodigal step-sisters,
in tight with *Incest* and …
pardon my laughter,
I hound my independence,
a short remote hilarity.

A Grim Depletion, 1819

Mary rolling in the sand;
a small sealed box in grass by the beach

How our planet withstands
the many lives
roiling the lithe hopes of restoration
and overcoming the conquests
for comfort
hardly gets beyond
the hot stretching drop of
a memory, I ready for,
like any desert
under the anxious widening
shadow of a meteor.

I once was such a planet.
Before the exile
and confinements,
before Death sat refreshed
upon a collection of
empty notches cradles set
in a circle around my still imagination,
my inability to seek,
a slack limited thought
finally lifting my chin
from my chest.
I resembled a slow rotation.
A partial orbit.

All the children were dead.
Our brave shunned circle
spun back to three,
like the day we left
the deft tongues of London,
the minds of parents
stricken with the ills of
debts and domination.

Our bright hated triad
stuck away stock moments,
clearly shedding the disbelief
we quietly carried throughout Italy
until our eyes had to speak,
so the moral hour they met
hardened in the mind,
trying me alone
for errors
I allowed to erect
the blasted cell of a love
our lives began to pace.

William, 1819

Mary holding her breath underwater;
a small sealed box floating above her

His blue eyes
rivalled the skies of Rome
in my failing arms
before the thin moist lids
weakened,
fell slowly,
woke the end's echo.

His molten halo of hair
long set in shapes
the heaving sea forms
as fingers pinch skin
chilled,
briefly spastic,
stowing the son's myth.

And then ...
What was our Italy?

Shelley,
the only father,
afterwards at the Baths
bound to
his Prometheus, unreachable,
ready to reside in
the Imagination's tacit consent,
alone,
private,
like any parent chasing a child.

Clara, 1818

Mary floating on her back;
a small sealed box in one hand

From the one cast as father
your features came,
my baby,
fair and free,
second of the daughters to escape,
to choose other than
a mere year or little more
among the Living—
all of us alive
for the Imagination,
a circle of chagrin
and shrieks,
an odd, antsy family.

You chose to avoid recovery
from the travels.

Our trio a trickery,
obeying his *orders*
one Venice spring;
I counted,
breaths first,
the flies at each nostril,
how the fleeing eyes harassed
a single anxious ray
into the face's centre,
and I saw the mother's hand:
a thumb,
two ink-trailed fingers
rolling the fair lock
we were to place
with the year's first yellow petals.

After Reading The 3rd Canto Of Byron's *Childe Harold*, 1817

Mary hidden behind a boulder;
a small sealed box on top of it

When the excursions made thought
seem last
and needless
the Intellectual rose rested
in the evening's crawl
— is the Summer's forever,
forgotten,
more to memory's pace,
how the mind displays
life dimming to dream?

In a furtive year
after pain felt new
and yearnful
the comparison began
based on the body's cracks
— is the Woman's wider,
longer,
due to love's trust,
how it supplies her heart
with instant answers?

All this *escape*
I blame on
dear ecstatic Albe!
Few have the scenes of
his smile kept for greetings;
I relive the lake leading
our early easy boat,
how the shore held still
with his vivid welcomes.

Dedication Revisited, 1817

> *Mary studying the sky:*
> *a small sealed box left behind on a boulder*

And now *my* heart
has no home,
the Summer tasks meant for two,
Percy,
unended,
left for the new widow I'll be.

Islam still Islam
in our last house,
Casa Magni,
where the mind's beauty boded
how to love
in the live circle we were.

Each cloud like each wave
clings to the moon.
I knew the stars with him—
what a thought,
what a truth—
not a twinkle grieves our gaze.

Between my toes
the sea brings a brief reunion,
the brother Laon,
the sister Cythna,
the Lovers
—we laughed as
the rumours toured England!

"A League of Incest!"
How ridiculous, how wrong.

The Memory no less
a lit thing of distant space
becomes the sight,
the Future's view too soon.

Where is the Past?
My murderous act?
Finally it feels ready to confess,
coldly rising in my dress,
this sea,
in need.

I sought sleep.

The Prosperous Friction, 1816

Mary seated against a boulder;
a small sealed box in her lap

Testimony waits
behind the tongue in thoughts
—such a sudden return to insight—
anxious,
for the air,
the unpredictable destiny of speech,
my brittle senses' version of
their little bond
witnessed, I hear,
the day Byron's lip quivered.

A trembling finger rests
on the undeniable log;
others were chosen
to burn my Percy's body,
gathered by our close fold,
relieved, able to move
both selves & stoves
to this salty grove,
as of yet unstricken
with the yarns of his exit.

Testimony?
Should I tell?
Yes!
I was present then.

When the candles snuffed themselves
I sought sleep;
listening in the midst of
the poet's verbal duel,
Byron,
on the Deity's side,

& Shelley,
on the Skeptic's.
I looked back once,
then the lamp bore a new hour
meant for the porous time
in such endless minds
beyond
the creeping futile line of morning's arrival.

A Hymn For A Hymn, 1816

Mary seated on a boulder;
a small sealed box in her arms

Break out the laughter for thoughts on Permanence.

The body's wish to conquer,
overturn, easily erase
that final & trusted appearance,

                the One
our shrunken circle saw as us:
as uncommonly solid:
as loyalty's proof—

              the mind opposes its own beauty!

Seal up the rupture & cracks lengthening in Love.

The eyes' curse to recede,
surrender, kindly kindle
that unseen & awful shadow,

               the Mystery
our current gloom dissolves in us:
in July's desertions:
in ecstasy's clasp—

            the heart firms its own form!

Loveliness, full of awe, bring no words;
we end, one known by the needs of air,
and him, the sea's bright child, free of vows.

Humankind, what a strange spell!

The Unnamed Daughter, 1815

Mary sitting on the sea's floor;
a small sealed box floating above her

London,
where the exile began
in the high window's
last image,
what the sun left for my gaze
cast by eyes
evincing the baby's calm.

The baby,
how the cornea greens
in this low murk's
gonging distance —
I resee yours
as the years sink
within the ray's
bright immersed quiver.

Memory,
when the clarity broke
in the first candle's
stiff gloom,
a tiny pulse over
before Dawn,
freed as mother
marks the still vein.

The body,
what the breast mourns
in this false womb's
ebbing plot;

I rehold you
before your father returns,
faced with
folding
his child's vacant arms.

A Season At Bishopsgate, 1815

Mary standing on a boulder;
a small sealed box between her feet

One brief and tranquil summer
I was led
to pardon the timing of fate
as shade went away
from the shadow,
bringing the hot spotted rooms
of Bishopsgate
where the white beams of
each ceiling smiled;
from this height
dusk plummets & ignites
as distance narrows quickly
to a lone house
taken without hesitancy
to remain Scandal's family.

I forget ...
as shade went away from the shadow?
Tis it!
The memory again grants my entry,
layers of daylight lower
into the sun's iris,
on the air appears
my Percy's sad cooing Aziola,
come to fuse
a pair of opposite seasons;

my soles accept the glacier's need
to sharpen stone,
much I actually feel
begins in the foot,
atop this still & cracked example
of Time's skill.

I retrieve ...
layers of daylight lower into the sea's iris?
Was it!
We took this same hour
On the water,
a quick quiet trip
to find the forest in reflections,
grief had not grown
to the size of the creature
in me today,
our minds adrift
in the love of Awe;
if I were to leap
the only reason could be clear
such a short fall
far too fair to satisfy,
left to go on,
the lost figurehead of the Don Juan.

In The Dim Limbo, 1814

Mary crouching at the sea's edge;
a small sealed box between her feet

Today the view grants a visit
to mother's grave
as hoarse waves
alter the hour,
& my awe of the sea's greed
found in the erasure of
an exiled footprint
coaxes the fearsome memory—
on the trees hung
my father's stalking eyes,
everywhere,
acting like leaves.

In the waggish home
he wrote for us
tears were untenable,
such a show
was thought to be beneath us,
a weakness
he, with his famous mind,
found vain—
for others—
not a Godwin.

I accept what the sea wishes,
the memory of my mother,
how I sat
in that patient churchyard
hearing the voice
she sent
up through the soil,

as if a brief approval,
the fierce reminder
of her revolt
also in my veins.

The Choice Revisited, 1814

Mary kneeling in the surf;
a small sealed box under a wave

And little of life
becomes light enough to let go!

Quite, yes, quite easy
to exasperate the sea:
I know it knows
I intend to toss back
the moment
I stepped into his carriage
unaware of
the white hours
awoken for us,
eager, too eager,
to lead the future forward
to the flow of sights
foraging in my mind,
aiding his bright grip,
his eyes' confident ache,
the love-led tug I saw
seat our dreams to dare.

And little of life
becomes light enough to let go!

To quit the jeers
looming on London's tongue
we nodded,
three isolated faces,
three wild pupils,
setting off the whip's triumphant crack
as dawn confirmed
the choice to explore
the edge of the Continent;

run with him
running from the one long charmed
by the constant *loiterous* option
suicide offered,
flooding her gravid body,
her eyes' endless vigil
the inexorable glare I watch
in this inhuman water.

And little of life
becomes light enough to let go!

Compared to any river
how the dawn did soothe!
We clapped as the clement sun
grew like a blessing
the kind window
keenly formed on the carriage floor,
a slow white shaft
warming our fated shoes,
& the defiant smiles we donned
before a bump shook
my mind back to Skinner St.
where father slept
without *her*,
the daughter I had left to him,
when at Dover we
drew up a will for the Past.

The Mule, 1814

Mary lying in the surf;
a small sealed box on her belly

I

Now, as the Continent remains
the tryst we toured,
I dare to greet the clouds
with the eyes he cast to me
that culprit day in the beginning
when the roads were laughter
& miles of new study
until our dear used Ass
went lame between towns.
Buying the beast meant
Percy's proper tangled money,
my sight until then stood
within my father's wealth
much like it stoops today
when the sky is his mouth;
we shoved on,
a new triune,
with my drear sister, Claire,
caught in endless complaints
of the ugly swollen ears.

II

What was France that day,
pocked by Napoleon's pass?
Burnt farms,
peasants in beds full of fleas,
rife with dreams Peace rebuilds
before dawn fondly tilts;
the unamused Alps,
those dark heights
where History roams,
as the sun consigns our answer
tied to a cart.
An able stranger calms his gleaming team,
tight dust enters
the mule's shadow
falling on our stalled dreams,
with an offer the heat dangles,
talk & coins join
the brief shade,
beast for beast so it went
as we faced the wavering distance,
restored,
by a stream.

His long fingers on my stiff thigh.

Promises At The St. Pancras Churchyard, 1814

Mary standing in the surf;
a small, sealed box floating at her feet

My other, Percy,
certainly respondent
& kindly
toward our usage of
the word *love*,
who declared it
like a taut vow,
two bound hairs
held to the sun.

His long fingers
on my stiff thigh,
gently clenching,
fingers the quill
had filled with
a frantic refutation
sceptical of God's
alleged existence.

My head hung
as his other hand
spoke to mine!

My thrill fell
through my lap
to the Future—
nothing but that moment
gazes back ...

We shared all we dared to.

No Other Heaven, 1812

Mary turning her back to the sea;
a small sealed box balanced on her palm:

Thinking,
apt endless venture,
curse or courage?

We were young before we met.
Before, as his early thoughts
asked about the Age,
about discrepancy,
that *between the will to do good*
& the power of doing so —
an Atheist's theory.

We were of no age
outside of a number.
Outside,
sitting apart,
under the sky's options,
a number of stars
to lead one to God,
or beyond
to Mab,
his hated fairy,
the queen he let reign.

"Doing good" never a strange notion,
within his reach,
closer to the hand,
he thought was possible
when he advocated
increasing the human power,
men's knowledge, then
there is no absolute need for Heaven,
or an afterlife.
He thought about us doing good.

How unlike my planted mind.
There is no other Heaven.
I say this knowing joy,
knowing I say words in favour of
that which is beyond the mind,
the men, their hands
waiting in the poor depths of pockets,
or held shut
by the inescapable sense of
a trusted prayer.

I gaze at the edge of Italy,
unable to forget
we shared all
we dared to,
the effort holy,
enough.

Acknowledgements

Some of these poems have appeared in the following publications:

Chapman Literary Quarterly (Scotland)
dANDelion (University of Calgary, Alberta)
Gaspereau Review (Nova Scotia)
Grain (Saskatchewan)
New Orphic Review (British Columbia)
Prairie Journal (Alberta)
Tasmanian Times (Australia)
Press Gang Journal (Nova Scotia)
Maple Tree Literary Supplement (Ontario)
Sentinel Journal (England)
Century 121 (Alaska)
The Quarterly Review (England)
Duane's PoeTree (Thailand)
Galway Review (Ireland)

Some of these poems have been read on: CFRO Co-Op Radio, Vancouver, BC

Thanks to: Ernest, Anne, Beth, Cuz Barb, Andrew, Joy, Jay

Big thanks to: June Scuddeler

Special big thanks to: Lainee

About the Author

Chad Norman continues to do things his way ... as any true poet must in the current age. His poems are published in countries around the globe. He continues to arrange/host events, helping other poets. His collection, *Selected & New Poems*, out from Mosaic Press, brings together 30 years of poems. Chad makes his home in Truro, Nova Scotia.

About the Illustrator

judith S bauer is a poet, painter, and sculptor of wild paper based in Parrsboro, Nova Scotia where she and her partner operate the Main & Station Nonesuch arts centre and residencies.

Other Works By Chad Norman

On The Urban Prairie & Other Shorter Poems (1986)
And If A Man Be Divided (1991)
Lives Of The Year (1994)
Standing In The Corner (1995)
The Breath Of One (1997)
What The Wind Brings (1999)
These Are My Elders (2001)
The Kulling (2001)
The Soft Furnace (2006)
Going Mad For The Love Of Sanity (2008)
There Is Music In The Word Impeachment (2009)
Ants On The Rainbow: Poems To, For, And About Children (2010)
Hugging The Huge Father (2011)
Hugging The Huge Father, Expanded Version (2012)
Masstown (2013)
Learning To Settle Down (2015)
Selected & New Poems (2017)